God's Blessing to y

on your graduation.

Pastor Chuck
+
Pastor Carol

Presented to:

_____

From:

_____

Date:

_____

Promises for the Graduate

PROMISES
FOR
THE
GRADUATE

Lawrence O. Richards

Daybreak Books

Zondervan Publishing House
Grand Rapids, Michigan

PROMISES FOR THE GRADUATE
previously published as The Believer's Promise Book
Copyright © 1982 by Lawrence O. Richards

Daybreak Books are published by
Zondervan Publishing House
1415 Lake Drive S.E.
Grand Rapids, MI 49506

Library of Congress Cataloging in Publication Data

Bible. English. New International. Selections. 1988.
  Promises for the graduate.

  Originally published under title: The believer's promise
book, c1982.
  Includes index.
  1. Bible—Indexes. I. Richards, Larry, 1931– .
II. Title.
BS195.N37 1988   220.5'2   88-76

Teal Edition: ISBN 0-310-39430-9
Gray Edition: ISBN 0-310-39440-6

Designed by Martha Manikas-Foster

Printed in the United States of America

91 92 93 94 95 96 97 / DH / 9 8 7 6 5 4 3 2

This edition is printed on acid-free paper and meets the Ameri-
can National Standards Institute Z39.48 standard.

Your relationship with God through Jesus
is very close and very special.
This book will help you
sense it more deeply,
for it brings together his promises,
helping you grasp:
your very personal relationship with God;
God's promises for your times of need;
and special prayers and God's answers.

CONTENTS

PART TWO:
God's Promises When You Are in Need

PART THREE:
Your Prayers . . . God's Answers

INTRODUCTION

Welcome to the adventure of life beyond graduation. As you take this significant step in your life—perhaps changing homes, cities, and friends—some very important principles in your life will *not* change, such as God's concern for you.

As a child of God, you are an inheritor of many wonderful promises. This book draws together great truths from the Old and the New Testament—truths that help you understand better God's commitment to you as his child.

There are three sections in this book, and in each section the verses are in random order, to avoid suggesting that a pattern of thought or teaching is being presented. The basic concept of this booklet is that Scripture provides a variety of insights for our particular needs, and that these insights should be allowed to stand on their own.

The first section, "Your Very Personal Relationship With God," is filled with wonderful truths, truths containing promises that are now yours in Christ.

When you feel uncertain, turn to this section and be refreshed by God's great love.

"God's Promises When You Are in Need" contains truths that speak to special needs. Perhaps you feel lonely or discouraged. Perhaps you're sick or nervous. Whatever your need, check the table of contents to find the page that shows you that God *does* care, and that he *will* care for you.

"Your Prayers . . . God's Answers" is filled with prayers uttered by Old and New Testament people and God's answers to their prayers. Prayer is one of your privileges as a member of God's family. You can share everything with God and be confident that he hears. This section will help you to express your feelings to God, and it will give you the assurance that God will answer you.

PART ONE

YOUR VERY PERSONAL
RELATIONSHIP WITH GOD

When you committed yourself to Jesus, God made a deep commitment to you. You are his now, and he wants to make the unchanging nature of his commitment to you clear. He wants you to be confident, so that "we who have fled to take hold of the hope offered to us may be greatly encouraged" (Hebrews 6:18).

The very hairs of your head are all numbered. So don't be afraid; you are worth more than many sparrows. *Matthew 10:30-31*

"You my sheep, the sheep of my pasture, are people, and I am your God," declares the Sovereign Lord. *Ezekiel 34:31*

Fear not, for I have redeemed you; I have called you by name; you are mine. *Isaiah 43:1*

My unfailing love for you will not be shaken nor my covenant of peace be removed. *Isaiah 54:10*

I have loved you with an everlasting love; I have drawn you with loving-kindness. I will build you up again. *Jeremiah 31:3-4*

I am concerned for you and will look on you with favor. *Ezekiel 36:9*

Know that the Lord has set apart the godly for himself; the Lord will hear when I call to him.
Psalm 4:3

He cares for those who trust in him.
Nahum 1:7

He will take great delight in you, he will quiet you with his love, he will rejoice over you with singing. *Zephaniah 3:17*

God sends his love and his faithfulness.
Psalm 57:3

I will not take my love from him, nor will I ever betray my faithfulness.

Psalm 89:33

For God so loved the world that he gave his one and only Son, that whoever believes in him shall not perish but have eternal life.

John 3:16

"They will be mine," says the Lord Almighty, "in the day when I make up my treasured possession."

Malachi 3:17

To all who received him, to those who believed in his name, he gave the right to become children of God.
John 1:12

Whoever believes in the Son has eternal life, but whoever rejects the Son will not see life, for God's wrath remains on him. *John 3:36*

Whoever hears my word and believes him who sent me has eternal life and will not be condemned; he has crossed over from death to life. *John 5:24*

I give them eternal life, and they shall never perish; no one can snatch them out of my hand.
John 10:28

Believe in the Lord Jesus, and you will be saved—you and your household. *Acts 16:31*

God has given us eternal life, and this life is in his Son. He who has the Son has life; he who does not have the Son of God does not have life.
1 John 5:11-12

He is able to save completely those who come to God through him, because he always lives to intercede for them. *Hebrews 7:25*

He who believes has everlasting life.
John 6:47

In him we have redemption through his blood, the forgiveness of sins, in accordance with the riches of God's grace. *Ephesians 1:7*

As the Scripture says, "Everyone who trusts in him will never be put to shame." For there is no difference between Jew and Gentile—the same Lord is Lord of all and richly blesses all who call on him, for "Everyone who calls on the name of the Lord will be saved."   *Romans 10:11-13*

You forgave the iniquity of your people and covered all their sins. *Psalm 85:2*

You are kind and forgiving, O Lord, abounding in love to all who call to you. *Psalm 86:5*

He forgives all my sins and heals all my diseases.
Psalm 103:3

As far as the east is from the west, so far has he removed our transgressions from us. As a father has compassion on his children, so the Lord has compassion on those who fear him; for he knows how we are formed, he remembers that we are dust.
Psalm 103:12-14

I acknowledged my sin to you and did not cover up my iniquity. I said, "I will confess my transgressions to the Lord"—and you forgave the guilt of my sin. *Psalm 32:5*

I will forgive their wickedness and will remember their sins no more. *Jeremiah 31:34*

If we confess our sins, he is faithful and just and will forgive us our sins and purify us from all unrighteousness. *1 John 1:9*

Who is a God like you, who pardons sin and forgives the transgression of the remnant of his inheritance? You do not stay angry forever but delight to show mercy. You will again have compassion on us; you will tread our sins underfoot and hurl all our iniquities into the depths of the sea. *Micah 7:18-19*

Everyone who believes in him receives forgiveness of sins through his name. *Acts 10:43*

21

Everyone who sins is a slave to sin. Now a slave has no permanent place in the family, but a son belongs to it forever. So if the Son sets you free, you will be free indeed. *John 8:34-36*

When you were slaves to sin, you were free from the control of righteousness. . . . But now that you have been set free from sin and have become slaves to God, the benefit you reap leads to holiness, and the result is eternal life. *Romans 6:20, 22*

Our old self was crucified with him so that the body of sin might be rendered powerless, that we should no longer be slaves to sin. *Romans 6:6*

Sin shall not be your master, because you are not under law, but under grace. *Romans 6:14*

Because of his great love for us, God, who is rich in mercy, made us alive with Christ even when we were dead in transgressions—it is by grace you have been saved. And God raised us up with Christ and seated us with him in the heavenly realms in Christ Jesus, in order that in the coming ages he might show the incomparable riches of his grace, expressed in his kindness to us in Christ Jesus. . . . For we are God's workmanship, created in Christ Jesus to do good works, which God prepared in advance for us to do. *Ephesians 2:4-7, 10*

No one who is born of God will continue to sin, because God's seed remains in him; he cannot go on sinning, because he has been born of God. *1 John 3:9*

The gospel . . . is the power of God for the salvation of everyone who believes. *Romans 1:16*

We, who with unveiled faces all reflect the Lord's glory, are being transformed into his likeness with ever-increasing glory, which comes from the Lord, who is the Spirit. *2 Corinthians 3:18*

He who began a good work in you will carry it on to completion until the day of Christ Jesus.

Philippians 1:6

Like newborn babies, crave pure spiritual milk, so that by it you may grow up in your salvation, now that you have tasted that the Lord is good. As you come to him, the living Stone . . . you also, like living stones, are being built into a spiritual house to be a holy priesthood, offering spiritual sacrifices acceptable to God through Jesus Christ. *1 Peter 2:2-5*

Speaking the truth in love, we will in all things grow up into him who is the Head, that is, Christ. From him the whole body, joined and held together by every supporting ligament, grows and builds itself up in love, as each part does its work.

Ephesians 4:15-16

He has given us his very great and precious promises, so that through them you may participate in the divine nature and escape the corruption in the world caused by evil desires. For this very reason, make every effort to add to your faith goodness; and to goodness, knowledge; and to knowledge, self-control; and to self-control, perseverance; and to perseverance, godliness; and to godliness, brotherly kindness; and to brotherly kindness, love. For if you possess these qualities in increasing measure, thcy will keep you from being ineffective and unproductive in your knowledge of our Lord Jesus Christ.   *2 Peter 1:4-8*

You, O Lord, are our Father, our Redeemer from of old is your name. *Isaiah 63:16*

I will be a Father to you, and you will be my sons and daughters. *2 Corinthians 6:18*

You are all sons of God through faith in Christ Jesus. *Galatians 3:26*

Whoever acknowledges the Son has the Father also. *1 John 2:23*

As a father has compassion on his children, so the Lord has compassion on those who fear him.
Psalm 103:13

The Father himself loves you because you have loved me and have believed that I came from God.
John 16:27

Jesus said, "I am returning to my Father and your Father, to my God and your God." *John 20:17*

Endure hardship as discipline; God is treating you as sons. For what son is not disciplined by his father? If you are not disciplined (and everyone undergoes discipline), then you are illegitimate children and not true sons. Moreover, we have all had human fathers who disciplined us and we respected them for it. How much more should we submit to the Father of our spirits and live! Our fathers disciplined us for a little while as they thought best; but God disciplines us for our good, that we may share in his holiness.
Hebrews 12:7-10

Every good and perfect gift is from above, coming down from the Father . . . who does not change like shifting shadows. *James 1:17*

I will discipline you, but only with justice.
Jeremiah 30:11

Know then in your heart that as a man disciplines his son, so the Lord your God disciplines you.
Deuteronomy 8:5

God disciplines us for our good, that we may share in his holiness. *Hebrews 12:10*

No discipline seems pleasant at the time, but painful. Later on, however, it produces a harvest of righteousness and peace for those who have been trained by it. *Hebrews 12:11*

Blessed is the man you discipline, O Lord, the man you teach from your law; you grant him relief from days of trouble, till a pit is dug for the wicked. For the Lord will not reject his people; he will never forsake his inheritance. *Psalm 94:12-14*

My son, do not despise the Lord's discipline and do not resent his rebuke, because the Lord disciplines those he loves, as a father the son he delights in.
Proverbs 3:11-12

Those whom I love I rebuke and discipline.
Revelation 3:19

When we are judged by the Lord, we are being disciplined so that we will not be condemned with the world. *1 Corinthians 11:32*

For these commands are a lamp, this teaching is a light, and the corrections of discipline are the way to life. *Proverbs 6:23*

He who spares the rod hates his son, but he who loves him is careful to discipline him.   *Proverbs 13:24*

God made him who had no sin to be sin for us, so that in him we might become the righteousness of God.

2 Corinthians 5:21

His divine power has given us everything we need for life and godliness through our knowledge of him.   *2 Peter 1:3*

Consecrate yourselves and be holy, because I am the Lord your God. Keep my decrees and follow them. I am the Lord, who makes you holy.   *Leviticus 20:7-8*

He chose us in him before the creation of the world to be holy and blameless in his sight.

Ephesians 1:4

Christ loved the church and gave himself up for her to make her holy, cleansing her by the washing with water through the word, and to present her to himself as a radiant church, without stain or wrinkle or any other blemish.   *Ephesians 5:25-27*

May he strengthen your hearts so that you will be blameless and holy in the presence of our God and Father when our Lord Jesus comes with all his holy ones.   *1 Thessalonians 3:13*

It is God's will that you should be sanctified.

1 Thessalonians 4:3

Command them to do good, to be rich in good deeds, and to be generous and willing to share. In this way they will lay up treasure for themselves as a firm foundation for the coming age, so that they may take hold of the life that is truly life.

1 Timothy 6:18-19

We know that anyone born of God does not continue to sin; the one who was born of God keeps him safe, and the evil one does not touch him.

1 John 5:18

The Lord Almighty is with us; the God of Jacob is our fortress. *Psalm 46:7*

From everlasting to everlasting the Lord's love is with those who fear him. *Psalm 103:17*

Neither death nor life, neither angels nor demons, neither the present nor the future, nor any powers, neither height nor depth, nor anything else in all creation, will be able to separate us from the love of God that is in Christ Jesus our Lord. *Romans 8:38-39*

The Lord is with us. *Numbers 14:9*

Be strong and courageous. Do not be afraid or terrified because of them, for the Lord your God goes with you; he will never leave you nor forsake you. *Deuteronomy 31:6*

Though my father and mother forsake me, the Lord will receive me. *Psalm 27:10*

I am always with you; you hold me by my right hand. *Psalm 73:23*

Surely I will be with you always, to the very end of the age. *Matthew 28:20*

All that the Father gives me will come to me, and whoever comes to me I will never drive away. For I have come down from heaven not to do my will but to do the will of him who sent me. And this is the will of him who sent me, that I shall lose none of all that he has given me, but raise them up at the last day. *John 6:37-39*

I, the God of Israel, will not forsake them. *Isaiah 41:17*

The Lord will not reject his people. *Psalm 94:14*

For the Lord your God is the one who goes with you to fight for you against your enemies to give you victory.
Deuteronomy 20:4

It is not by sword or spear that the Lord saves; for the battle is the Lord's.
1 Samuel 17:47

He is your praise; he is your God, who performed for you those great and awesome wonders you saw with your own eyes.
Deuteronomy 10:21

In you our fathers put their trust; they trusted and you delivered them. They cried to you and were saved; in you they trusted and were not disappointed.
Psalm 22:4-5

The Lord is the everlasting God, the Creator of the ends of the earth. He will not grow tired or weary, and his understanding no one can fathom. He gives strength to the weary and increases the power of the weak.
Isaiah 40:28-29

You are the God who performs miracles.
Psalm 77:14

I am the Lord, your God, who takes hold of your right hand and says to you, Do not fear; I will help you.
Isaiah 41:13

He raises the poor from the dust and lifts the needy from the ash heap; he seats them with princes and has them inherit a throne of honor. For the foundations of the earth are the Lord's; upon them he has set the world. He will guard the feet of his saints.
1 Samuel 2:8-9

For the Lord is our judge; the Lord is our lawgiver; the Lord is our king, it is he who will save us.

Isaiah 33:22

Ask and it will be given to you; seek and you will find; knock and the door will be opened to you.

Matthew 7:7

Everyone who asks receives; he who seeks finds; and to him who knocks, the door will be opened.

Matthew 7:8

The eyes of the Lord are on the righteous and his ears are attentive to their prayer.   *1 Peter 3:12*

I will do whatever you ask in my name, so that the Son may bring glory to the Father.   *John 14:13*

You may ask me for anything in my name, and I will do it.   *John 14:14*

If we ask anything according to his will, he hears us. And if we know that he hears us—whatever we ask—we know that we have what we asked of him.

1 John 5:14-15

Know that the Lord has set apart the godly for himself; the Lord will hear when I call to him.

Psalm 4:3

Which of you, if his son asks for bread, will give him a stone? Or if he asks for a fish, will give him a snake? If you, then, though you are evil, know how to give good gifts to your children, how much more will your Father in heaven give good gifts to those who ask him!   *Matthew 7:9-11*

O you who hear prayer, to you all men will come. . . . You answer us with awesome deeds of righteousness, O God our Savior.   *Psalm 65:2, 5*

Surely the arm of the Lord is not too short to save, nor his ear too dull to hear. *Isaiah 59:1*

In your unfailing love you will lead the people you have redeemed. In your strength you will guide them to your holy dwelling. *Exodus 15:13*

I will help you speak and will teach you what to say. *Exodus 4:12*

Whether you turn to the right or to the left, your ears will hear a voice behind you, saying, "This is the way; walk in it." *Isaiah 30:21*

The Lord gives wisdom, and from his mouth come knowledge and understanding. *Proverbs 2:6*

I will instruct you and teach you in the way you should go. *Psalm 32:8*

The Holy Spirit, whom the Father will send in my name, will teach you all things and will remind you of everything I have said to you. *John 14:26*

It is the Spirit in a man, the breath of the Almighty, that gives him understanding. It is not only the old who are wise, nor only the aged who understand what is right. *Job 32:8,9*

You guide me with your counsel, and afterward you will take me into glory. *Psalm 73:24*

The secret things belong to the Lord our God, but the things revealed belong to us and to our children forever, that we may follow all the words of this law. *Deuteronomy 29:29*

I will give you words and wisdom that none of your adversaries will be able to resist or contradict. *Luke 21:15*

When he, the Spirit of truth, comes, he will guide you into all truth. *John 16:13*

Even on my servants, both men and women, I will pour out my Spirit in those days. *Joel 2:29*

Whoever believes in me, as the Scripture has said, streams of living water will flow from within him. By this he meant the Spirit, whom those who believed in him were later to receive. *John 7:38-39*

I will ask the Father, and he will give you another Counselor to be with you forever—the Spirit of truth.
John 14:16-17

If the Spirit of him who raised Jesus from the dead is living in you, he who raised Christ from the dead will also give life to your mortal bodies through his Spirit, who lives in you. *Romans 8:11*

Your body is a temple of the Holy Spirit, who is in you. *1 Corinthians 6:19*

The one who is in you is greater than the one who is in the world. *1 John 4:4*

The Lord gives strength to his people; the Lord blesses his people with peace. *Psalm 29:11*

I stay close to you; your right hand upholds me.
Psalm 63:8

[God] is able to do immeasurably more than all we ask or imagine, according to his power that is at work within us. *Ephesians 3:20*

My hand will sustain him; surely my arm will strengthen him. *Psalm 89:21*

Surely God is my salvation; I will trust and not be afraid. The Lord, the Lord, is my strength and my song; he has become my salvation. *Isaiah 12:2*

As for God, his way is perfect; the word of the Lord is flawless. He is a shield for all who take refuge in him. *2 Samuel 22:31; Psalm 18:30*

The Lord helps them and delivers them; he delivers them from the wicked and saves them, because they take refuge in him. *Psalm 37:40*

"Because he loves me," says the Lord, "I will rescue him; I will protect him, for he acknowledges my name." *Psalm 91:14*

The Lord protects the simplehearted.
Psalm 116:6

My help comes from the Lord, the Maker of heaven and earth. He will not let your foot slip—he who watches over you will not slumber.
Psalm 121:2-3

"I will watch over them to build and to plant," declares the Lord. *Jeremiah 31:28*

He will cover you with his feathers, and under his wings you will find refuge; his faithfulness will be your shield and rampart. *Psalm 91:4*

If you make the Most High your dwelling—even the Lord, who is my refuge—then no harm will befall you, no disaster will come near. *Psalm 91:9-10*

The Lord preserves the faithful. *Psalm 31:23*

I know whom I have believed, and am convinced that he is able to guard what I have entrusted to him for that day. *2 Timothy 1:12*

For the Lord loves the just and will not forsake his faithful ones. They will be protected forever.

Psalm 37:28

Lord, you will keep us safe and protect us . . . forever.

Psalm 12:7

God is able to make all grace abound to you, so that in all things at all times, having all you need, you will abound in every good work.   *2 Corinthians 9:8*

The Lord will guide you always; he will satisfy your needs in a sun-scorched land and will strengthen your frame.   *Isaiah 58:11*

When you have eaten and are satisfied, praise the Lord your God for the good land he has given you.

Deuteronomy 8:10

The Lord is my shepherd, I shall lack nothing.

Psalm 23:1

Remember the Lord your God, for it is he who gives you the ability to produce wealth.

Deuteronomy 8:18

He is our God and we are the people of his pasture, the flock under his care.   *Psalm 95:7*

Surely God is my help; the Lord is the one who sustains me.   *Psalm 54:4*

Yours, O Lord, is the kingdom, you are exalted as head over all. Wealth and honor come from you; you are the ruler of all things. In your hands are strength and power to exalt and give strength to all.

1 Chronicles 29:11-12

I tell you, do not worry about your life, what you will eat or drink; or about your body, what you will wear. Is not life more important than food, and the body more important than clothes? Look at the birds of the air; they do not sow or reap or store away in barns, and yet your heavenly Father feeds them. Are you not much more valuable than they?

Matthew 6:25-26

God will meet all your needs.

Philippians 4:19

I will put my law in their minds and write it on their hearts.
Jeremiah 31:33

You are a letter from Christ, the result of our ministry, written not with ink but with the Spirit of the living God, not on tablets of stone but on tablets of human hearts.
2 Corinthians 3:3

The blood of Christ, who through the eternal Spirit offered himself unblemished to God, [will] cleanse our consciences from acts that lead to death, so that we may serve the living God!
Hebrews 9:14

This is what the Lord has commanded you to do, so that the glory of the Lord may appear to you.
Leviticus 9:6

Whoever has my commands and obeys them, he is the one who loves me.
John 14:21

If anyone loves me, he will obey my teaching. My Father will love him, and we will come to him and make our home with him. He who does not love me will not obey my teaching.
John 14:23-24

No one who lives in him keeps on sinning.
1 John 3:6

This is love for God: to obey his commands. And his commands are not burdensome, for everyone born of God has overcome the world. . . . Who is it that overcomes the world? Only he who believes that Jesus is the Son of God.
1 John 5:3-5

I have chosen the way of truth; I have set my heart on your laws. I hold fast to your statutes, O Lord; do not let me be put to shame. I run in the path of your commands, for you have set my heart free.

Psalm 119:30-32

I will send down showers in season; there will be showers of blessing. *Ezekiel 34:26*

He who did not spare his own Son, but gave him up for us all—how will he not also, along with him, graciously give us all things? *Romans 8:32*

Praise be to the God and Father of our Lord Jesus Christ, who has blessed us in the heavenly realm with every spiritual blessing in Christ. *Ephesians 1:3*

How great is your goodness, which you have stored up for those who fear you, which you bestow in the sight of men on those who take refuge in you.

Psalm 31:19

God will bless us, and all the ends of the earth will fear him. *Psalm 67:7*

Blessed are those whose strength is in you.

Psalm 84:5

The Lord will indeed give what is good.

Psalm 85:12

He satisfies the thirsty and fills the hungry with good things. *Psalm 107:9*

He will bless those who fear the Lord—small and great alike. *Psalm 115:13*

Tell the righteous it will be well with them, for they will enjoy the fruit of their deeds. *Isaiah 3:10*

Blessed are all who fear the Lord, who walk in his ways. *Psalm 128:1*

Blessed is the man who trusts in the Lord, whose confidence is in him. *Jeremiah 17:7*

The Lord remembers us and will bless us.

Psalm 115:12

I will never stop doing good to them.

Jeremiah 32:40

I the Lord search the heart and examine the mind, to reward a man according to his conduct.

Jeremiah 17:10

Your Father, who sees what is done in secret, will reward you.

Matthew 6:4

At the renewal of all things . . . everyone who has left houses or brothers or sisters or father or mother or children or fields for my sake will receive a hundred times as much and will inherit eternal life.

Matthew 19:28-29

My Father will honor the one who serves me.

John 12:26

You will receive an inheritance from the Lord as a reward.

Colossians 3:24

Now there is in store for me the crown of righteousness, which the Lord, the righteous Judge, will award to me on that day—and not only to me, but also to all who have longed for his appearing.

2 Timothy 4:8

The Lord has dealt with me according to my righteousness; according to the cleanness of my hands he has rewarded me.

2 Samuel 22:21

In his great mercy he has given us new birth into a living hope through the resurrection of Jesus Christ from the dead, and into an inheritance that can never perish, spoil or fade—kept in heaven for you, who through faith are shielded by God's power until the coming of the salvation that is ready to be revealed in the last time.

1 Peter 1:3-5

When the Chief Shepherd appears, you will receive the crown of glory that will never fade.

1 Peter 5:4

Blessed are the peacemakers, for they will be called sons of God.   *Matthew 5:9*

If anyone gives a cup of cold water to one of these little ones because he is my disciple, I tell you the truth, he will certainly not lose his reward.   *Matthew 10:42*

To each one the manifestation of the Spirit is given for the common good.   *1 Corinthians 12:7*

As for me, far be it from me that I should sin against the Lord by failing to pray for you. And I will teach you the way that is good and right.

1 Samuel 12:23

Blessed is he who has regard for the weak; the Lord delivers him in times of trouble.   *Psalm 41:1*

Good will come to him who is generous and lends freely.   *Psalm 112:5*

He who is kind to the poor lends to the Lord, and he will reward him for what he has done. *Proverbs 19:17*

A despairing man should have the devotion of his friends.   *Job 6.14*

Praise be to the God . . . of all comfort, who comforts us in all our troubles, so that we can comfort those in any trouble with the comfort we ourselves have received from God.   *2 Corinthians 1:3-4*

Our competence comes from God. He has made us competent as ministers of a new covenant.

2 Corinthians 3:5-6

Each one should use whatever gift he has received to serve others, faithfully administering God's grace in its various forms.   *1 Peter 4:10*

The Lord God said, "It is not good for the man to be alone. I will make a helper suitable for him." . . . Then the Lord God made a woman from the rib he had taken out of the man, and he brought her to the man.

Genesis 2:18, 22

Love your neighbor as yourself.   *Mark 12:31*

Love one another. As I have loved you, so you must love one another. All men will know that you are my disciples if you love one another.

John 13:34-35

Let no debt remain outstanding, except the continuing debt to love one another, for he who loves his fellow man has fulfilled the law.   *Romans 13:8*

May the God who gives endurance and encouragement give you a spirit of unity among yourselves as you follow Christ Jesus, so that with one heart and mouth you may glorify the God and Father of our Lord Jesus Christ.   *Romans 15:5-6*

Where two or three come together in my name, there am I with them.   *Matthew 18:20*

You are all one in Christ Jesus.

Galatians 3:28

How can we thank God enough for you in return for all the joy we have in the presence of our God because of you?   *1 Thessalonians 3:9*

May the Lord make your love increase and overflow for each other and for everyone else.

1 Thessalonians 3:12

Now that you have purified yourselves by obeying the truth so that you have sincere love for your brothers, love one another deeply, from the heart.

1 Peter 1:22

For I have chosen him, so that he will direct his children and his household after him to keep the way of the Lord by doing what is right and just.   *Genesis 18:19*

So will I save you, and you will be a blessing.

Zechariah 8:13

If you repent, I will restore you that you may serve me.   *Jeremiah 15:19*

"Come, follow me," Jesus said, "and I will make you fishers of men."   *Matthew 4:19*

Anyone who has faith in me will do what I have been doing. He will do even greater things than these, because I am going to the Father.   *John 14:12*

I thank Christ Jesus our Lord, who has given me strength, that he considered me faithful, appointing me to his service.   *1 Timothy 1:12*

He whose walk is blameless will minister to me.

Psalm 101:6

[Jesus] has made us to be a kingdom and priests to serve his God and Father.   *Revelation 1:6*

Whoever wants to become great among you must be your servant, and whoever wants to be first must be your slave—just as the Son of Man did not come to be served, but to serve, and to give his life as a ransom for many.   *Matthew 20:26-28*

This is to my Father's glory, that you bear much fruit, showing yourselves to be my disciples.   *John 15:8*

There are different kinds of gifts, but the same Spirit. There are different kinds of service, but the same Lord.   *1 Corinthians 12:4-5*

Since we have been justified through faith, we have peace with God through our Lord Jesus Christ, through whom we have gained access by faith into this grace in which we now stand. *Romans 5:1-2*

My Presence will go with you, and I will give you rest. *Exodus 33:14*

He promises peace to his people, his saints.
Psalm 85:8

Great peace have they who love your law, and nothing can make them stumble. *Psalm 119:165*

You will keep in perfect peace him whose mind is steadfast, because he trusts in you. *Isaiah 26:3*

The fruit of righteousness will be peace; the effect of righteousness will be quietness and confidence forever. *Isaiah 32:17*

Take my yoke upon you and learn from me, for I am gentle and humble in heart, and you will find rest for your souls. *Matthew 11:29*

He himself is our peace. *Ephesians 2:14*

Let the peace of Christ rule in your hearts, since as members of one body you were called to peace.
Colossians 3:15

Peace I leave with you; my peace I give you.
John 14:27

The Lord bless you and keep you; the Lord make his face shine upon you and be gracious to you; the Lord turn his face toward you and give you peace.
Numbers 6:24-26

Ask and you will receive, and your joy will be complete. *John 16:24*

May the righteous be glad and rejoice before God; may they be happy and joyful. *Psalm 68:3*

Satisfy us in the morning with your unfailing love, that we may sing for joy and be glad all our days. *Psalm 90:14*

You have made known to me the path of life; you will fill me with joy in your presence, with eternal pleasures at your right hand. *Psalm 16:11*

If you obey my commands, you will remain in my love, just as I have obeyed my Father's commands and remain in his love. I have told you this so that my joy may be in you, and that your joy may be complete. *John 15:10-11*

Everlasting joy will crown their heads. Gladness and joy will overtake them, and sorrow and sighing will flee away. *Isaiah 51:11*

Let us fix our eyes on Jesus, the author and perfecter of our faith, who for the joy set before him endured the cross, scorning its shame. *Hebrews 12:2*

You will rejoice, and no one will take away your joy. *John 16:22*

The joy of the Lord is your strength. *Nehemiah 8:10*

Light is shed upon the righteous and joy on the upright in heart. *Psalm 97:11*

May the God of hope fill you with all joy and peace as you trust in him. *Romans 15:13*

You believe in him and are filled with an inexpressible and glorious joy.   *1 Peter 1:8*

You are a chosen people, a royal priesthood, a holy nation, a people belonging to God, that you may declare the praises of him who called you out of darkness into his wonderful light. *1 Peter 2:9*

The Lord will fulfill his purpose for me.
Psalm 138:8

And now, O Israel, what does the Lord your God ask of you but to fear the Lord your God, to walk in all his ways, to love him, to serve the Lord your God with all your heart and with all your soul?
Deuteronomy 10:12

"For I know the plans I have for you," declares the Lord, "plans to prosper you and not to harm you, plans to give you hope and a future." *Jeremiah 29:11*

May our Lord Jesus Christ himself and God our Father, who loved us and by his grace gave us eternal encouragement and good hope, encourage your hearts and strengthen you in every good deed and word.
2 Thessalonians 2:16-17

God . . . will not forget your work and the love you have shown him as you have helped his people and continue to help them. *Hebrews 6:10*

Let your light shine before men, that they may see your good works and praise your Father in heaven.
Matthew 5:16

I want you to stress these things, so that those who have trusted in God may be careful to devote themselves to doing what is good. These things are excellent and profitable to everyone. *Titus 3:8*

If anyone serves, he should do so with the strength God provides, so that in all things God may be praised.

1 Peter 4:11

"I am coming, and I will live among you," declares the Lord. *Zechariah 2:10*

When Christ, who is your life, appears, then you also will appear with him in glory. *Colossians 3:4*

Christ was sacrificed once to take away the sins of many people; and he will appear a second time, not to bear sin, but to bring salvation to those who are waiting for him. *Hebrews 9:28*

He who is coming will come and will not delay. *Hebrews 10:37*

The Lord himself will come down from heaven, with a loud command, with the voice of the archangel and with the trumpet call of God, and the dead in Christ will rise first. After that, we who are still alive and are left will be caught up with them in the clouds to meet the Lord in the air. And so we will be with the Lord forever. *1 Thessalonians 4:16-17*

In my Father's house are many rooms; if it were not so, I would have told you. I am going there to prepare a place for you. And if I go and prepare a place for you, I will come back and take you to be with me that you also may be where I am. *John 14:2-3*

This same Jesus, who has been taken from you into heaven, will come back in the same way you have seen him go into heaven. *Acts 1:11*

We know that when he appears, we shall be like him, for we shall see him as he is. *1 John 3:2*

He is coming with the clouds, and every eye will see him, even those who pierced him. *Revelation 1:7*

The Son of Man will come. . . . *Matthew 24:44*

Everyone who looks to the Son and believes in him shall have eternal life, and I will raise him up at the last day. *John 6:40*

The one who raised the Lord Jesus from the dead will also raise us with Jesus and present us with you in his presence. *2 Corinthians 4:14*

The Lord Jesus Christ, who, by the power that enables him to bring everything under his control, will transform our lowly bodies so that they will be like his glorious body. *Philippians 3:20-21*

I know that my Redeemer lives, and that in the end he will stand upon the earth. And after my skin has been destroyed, yet in my flesh I will see God; I myself will see him with my own eyes—I, and not another. *Job 19:25-27*

But your dead will live; their bodies will rise. You who dwell in the dust, wake up and shout for joy. *Isaiah 26:19*

We will not all sleep, but we will all be changed . . . the dead will be raised imperishable, and we will be changed. *1 Corinthians 15:51-52*

If we have been united with him in his death, we will certainly also be united with him in his resurrection. *Romans 6:5*

When I awake, I will be satisfied with seeing your likeness. *Psalm 17:15*

I will ransom them from the power of the grave; I will redeem them from death. *Hosea 13:14*

The dead will hear the voice of the Son of God and those who hear will live.   *John 5:25*

PART TWO

GOD'S PROMISES WHEN YOU ARE IN NEED

Scripture speaks confidently. God loves you deeply, and he will meet all your needs. At times you have emotional needs, and God's Word brings calm. At times you need guidance, and his Word gives counsel. At times God works directly through circumstances or Christian brothers and sisters. Whatever the situation, God will give us comfort, counsel, and peace.

If anyone acknowledges that Jesus is the Son of God, God lives in him and he in God.   *1 John 4:15*

The Lord redeems his servants; no one who takes refuge in him will be condemned.   *Psalm 34:22*

He was delivered over to death for our sins and was raised to life for our justification.   *Romans 4:25*

It does not, therefore, depend on man's desire or effort, but on God's mercy.   *Romans 9:16*

With the Lord is unfailing love and with him is full redemption.   *Psalm 130:7*

Jesus said . . . , "I am the resurrection and the life. He who believes in me will live, even though he dies; and whoever lives and believes in me will never die."

John 11:25-26

All have sinned and fall short of the glory of God, and are justified freely by his grace through the redemption that came by Christ Jesus.   *Romans 3:23-24*

I have not come to call the righteous, but sinners.

Matthew 9:13

To all who received him, to those who believed in his name, he gave the right to become children of God.

John 1:12

To the man who does not work but trusts God who justifies the wicked, his faith is credited as righteousness.   *Romans 4:5*

Whoever believes in him is not condemned.

John 3:18

These are written that you may believe that Jesus is the Christ, the Son of God, and that by believing you may have life in his name.   *John 20:31*

You were washed, you were sanctified, you were justified in the name of the Lord Jesus Christ and by the Spirit of our God. *1 Corinthians 6:11*

In him and through faith in him we may approach God with freedom and confidence.

Ephesians 3:12

But you are a forgiving God, gracious and compassionate, slow to anger and abounding in love.

Nehemiah 9:17

If you, O Lord, kept a record of sins, O Lord, who could stand? But with you there is forgiveness.

Psalm 130:3-4

God does not take away life; instead, he devises ways so that a banished person may not remain estranged from him. *2 Samuel 14:14*

I, even I, am he who blots out your transgressions, for my own sake, and remembers your sins no more. *Isaiah 43:25*

The Lord our God is merciful and forgiving, even though we have rebelled against him. *Daniel 9:9*

Let the wicked forsake his way and the evil man his thoughts. Let him turn to the Lord, and he will have mercy on him. *Isaiah 55:7*

Blessed is the man whose sin the Lord does not count against him. *Psalm 32:2*

I will cleanse them from all the sin they have committed against me and will forgive all their sins of rebellion against me.

Jeremiah 33:8

I will not be angry forever. Only acknowledge
your guilt.   *Jeremiah 3:12*
Whoever believes in him is not condemned.
John 3:18

Do not be afraid. Stand firm and you will see the deliverance the Lord will bring you.   *Exodus 14:13*

I will strengthen you and help you; I will uphold you with my righteous right hand.   *Isaiah 41:10*

I do not even judge myself. . . . It is the Lord who judges me. Therefore judge nothing before the appointed time; wait till the Lord comes. He will bring to light what is hidden in darkness and will expose the motives of men's hearts. At that time each will receive his praise from God.   *1 Corinthians 4:3-5*

The Lord does not look at the things men look at. Man looks at the outward appearance, but the Lord looks at the heart.   *1 Samuel 16:7*

Stand firm. Let nothing move you. Always give yourselves fully to the work of the Lord, because you know that your labor in the Lord is not in vain.
      1 Corinthians 15:58

You need to persevere so that when you have done the will of God, you will receive what he has promised.   *Hebrews 10:36*

He will be the sure foundation for your times, a rich store of salvation and wisdom and knowledge.
      Isaiah 33:6

Who are you to judge someone else's servant? To his own master he stands or falls. And he will stand, for the Lord is able to make him stand.

      Romans 14:4

Have I not commanded you? Be strong and courageous. Do not be terrified; do not be discouraged, for the Lord your God will be with you wherever you go.   *Joshua 1:9*

Yours, O Lord, is the greatness and the power and the glory and the majesty and the splendor, for everything in heaven and earth is yours. Yours, O Lord, is the kingdom; you are exalted as head over all.
1 Chronicles 29:11

He satisfies the thirsty and fills the hungry with good things.
Psalm 107:9

God will meet all your needs according to his glorious riches in Christ Jesus.
Philippians 4:19

He provides food for those who fear him.
Psalm 111:5

Now he who supplies seed to the sower and bread for food will also supply and increase your store of seed and will enlarge the harvest of your righteousness. You will be made rich in every way so that you can be generous on every occasion.
2 Corinthians 9:10-11

He will deliver the needy who cry out, the afflicted who have no one to help.
Psalm 72:12

He who works his land will have abundant food.
Proverbs 28:19

There were no needy persons among them. For from time to time those who owned lands or houses sold them, brought the money from the sales and put it at the apostles' feet, and it was distributed to anyone as he had need.
Acts 4:34-35

Better the little that the righteous have than the wealth of many wicked.
Psalm 37:16

With righteousness he will judge the needy, with justice he will give decisions for the poor of the earth.

Isaiah 11:4

The Lord hears the needy.

Psalm 69:33

The Lord is my helper; I will not be afraid. What can man do to me? *Hebrews 13:6*

Do not be terrified, . . . for the Lord your God, who is among you, is a great and awesome God. *Deuteronomy 7:21*

For great is the Lord and most worthy of praise; he is to be feared above all gods. For all the gods of the nations are idols, but the Lord made the heavens. *1 Chronicles 16:25-26*

I am with you to rescue and save you. *Jeremiah 15:20*

So do not fear, for I am with you; do not be dismayed, for I am your God. *Isaiah 41:10*

When a man's ways are pleasing to the Lord, he makes even his enemies live at peace with him. *Proverbs 16:7*

Say to those with fearful hearts, "Be strong, do not fear; your God will come." *Isaiah 35:4*

He will deliver us. *2 Corinthians 1:10*

Whatever you have learned or received or heard from me, or seen in me—put it into practice. And the God of peace will be with you. *Philippians 4:9*

Don't be afraid of them. Remember the Lord, who is great and awesome. *Nehemiah 4:14*

The Lord is my strength and my shield; my heart trusts in him. *Psalm 28:7*

Do not be afraid of any man, for judgment belongs to God. *Deuteronomy 1:17*

The Lord will be a refuge for his people. *Joel 3:16*

I will lie down and sleep in peace, for you alone,
O Lord, make me dwell in safety.   *Psalm 4:8*
When I am afraid, I will trust in you.   *Psalm 56:3*

Come to me, all you who are weary and burdened, and I will give you rest. *Matthew 11:28*

In this world you will have trouble. But take heart! I have overcome the world. *John 16:33*

I am with you and will watch over you wherever you go, and I will bring you back to this land. I will not leave you until I have done what I have promised. *Genesis 28:15*

It is unthinkable that God would do wrong, that the Almighty would pervert justice. *Job 34:12*

Some trust in chariots and some in horses, but we trust in the name of the Lord our God. *Psalm 20:7*

Call upon me in the day of trouble; I will deliver you, and you will honor me. *Psalm 50:15*

Cast your cares on the Lord and he will sustain you. *Psalm 55:22*

In the day of my trouble I will call to you, for you will answer me. *Psalm 86:7*

I am the Lord, your God, who takes hold of your right hand and says to you, Do not fear; I will help you. *Isaiah 41:13*

Trust in the Lord with all your heart and lean not on your own understanding; in all your ways acknowledge him, and he will make your paths straight. *Proverbs 3:5-6*

He tends his flock like a shepherd: He gathers the lambs in his arms and carries them close to his heart; he gently leads those that have young. *Isaiah 40:11*

Praise be to the Lord, to God our Savior, who daily bears our burdens.   *Psalm 68:19*

He fulfills the desires of those who fear him.

Psalm 145:19

We constantly pray for you, that our God may count you worthy of his calling, and that by his power he may fulfill every good purpose of yours and every act prompted by your faith.   *2 Thessalonians 1:11*

Turn my eyes away from worthless things; renew my life according to your word.   *Psalm 119:37*

Commit to the Lord whatever you do, and your plans will succeed.   *Proverbs 16:3*

I know what it is to be in need, and I know what it is to have plenty. I have learned the secret of being content in any and every situation, whether well fed or hungry, whether living in plenty or in want. I can do everything through him who gives me strength.

Philippians 4:12-13

For the Lord God is a sun and shield; the Lord bestows favor and honor; no good thing does he withhold from those whose walk is blameless.

Psalm 84:11

In his heart a man plans his course, but the Lord determines his steps.   *Proverbs 16:9*

I said to the Lord, "You are my Lord; apart from you I have no good thing."   *Psalm 16:2*

He who works his land will have abundant food.

Proverbs 28:19

I am the bread of life. He who comes to me will never go hungry, and he who believes in me will never be thirsty.   *John 6:35*

He will teach us his ways, so that we may walk in his paths.

Micah 4:2

Blessed are those who mourn, for they will be comforted.   *Matthew 5:4*

I will cause all my goodness to pass in front of you, and I will proclaim my name, the Lord, in your presence. I will have mercy on whom I will have mercy, and I will have compassion on whom I will have compassion.   *Exodus 33:19*

Hope does not disappoint us, because God has poured out his love into our hearts by the Holy Spirit, whom he has given us.   *Romans 5:5*

I will give them comfort and joy instead of sorrow.   *Jeremiah 31:13*

I will not forget you.   *Isaiah 49:15*

May the God of hope fill you with all joy and peace as you trust in him, so that you may overflow with hope by the power of the Holy Spirit.

Romans 15:13

The Lord himself goes before you and will be with you; he will never leave nor forsake you. Do not be afraid; do not be discouraged.   *Deuteronomy 31:8*

Weeping may remain for a night, but rejoicing comes in the morning.   *Psalm 30:5*

With everlasting kindness I will have compassion on you.   *Isaiah 54:8*

Gladness and joy will overtake them, and sorrow and sighing will flee away.   *Isaiah 35:10*

Rejoice in the hope of the glory of God.

Romans 5:2

May your unfailing love be my comfort, according to your promise to your servant.   *Psalm 119:76*

Why are you downcast, O my soul? . . . Put your hope in God, for I will yet praise him.   *Psalm 42:11*

This is my prayer: that your love may abound more and more in knowledge and depth of insight, so that you may be able to discern what is best and may be pure and blameless. *Philippians 1:9-10*

Whoever follows me will never walk in darkness, but will have the light of life. *John 8:12*

If any of you lacks wisdom, he should ask God, who gives generously to all without finding fault, and it will be given to him. *James 1:5*

Teach me your way, O Lord, and I will walk in your truth. *Psalm 86:11*

I will lead them beside streams of water on a level path where they will not stumble.

Jeremiah 31:9

I know, O Lord, that a man's life is not his own; it is not for man to direct his steps.

Jeremiah 10:23

I will counsel you and watch over you.

Psalm 32:8

The spiritual man makes judgments about all things, but he himself is not subject to any man's judgment: "For who has known the mind of the Lord that he may instruct him?" But we have the mind of Christ. *1 Corinthians 2:15-16*

The Holy Spirit will teach you at that time what you should say. *Luke 12:12*

I will praise the Lord who counsels me; even at night my heart instructs me. *Psalm 16:7*

The entrance of your words gives light; it gives understanding to the simple. *Psalm 119:130*

Open my eyes that I may see wonderful things in your law. *Psalm 119:18*

Blessed are those who are persecuted because of righteousness, for theirs is the kingdom of heaven.

Matthew 5:10

You intended to harm me, but God intended it for good to accomplish what is now being done, the saving of many lives.

Genesis 50:20

I call to the Lord, who is worthy of praise, and I am saved from my enemies.

2 Samuel 22:4

I have set the Lord always before me. Because he is at my right hand, I will not be shaken.

Psalm 16:8

Many are the woes of the wicked, but the Lord's unfailing love surrounds the man who trusts in him.

Psalm 32:10

Do not fret because of evil men or be envious of those who do wrong; for like the grass they will soon wither, like green plants they will soon die away.

Psalm 37:1-2

The Lord works righteousness and justice for all the oppressed.

Psalm 103:6

He rescues the life of the needy from the hands of the wicked.

Jeremiah 20:13

He must turn from evil and do good; he must seek peace and pursue it. For the eyes of the Lord are on the righteous, and his ears are attentive to their prayer.

1 Peter 3:11-12

I will contend with those who contend with you, and your children I will save.

Isaiah 49:25

The scepter of the wicked will not remain over the land allotted to the righteous. *Psalm 125:3*

The oppressor will come to an end. *Isaiah 16:4*

God is faithful; he will not let you be tempted beyond what you can bear. But when you are tempted, he will also provide a way out so that you can stand up under it.   *1 Corinthians 10:13*

Live by the Spirit, and you will not gratify the desires of the sinful nature.

Galatians 5:16

He knows the way that I take; when he has tested me, I will come forth as gold.   *Job 23:10*

I gain understanding from your precepts; therefore I hate every wrong path.

Psalm 119:104

When tempted, no one should say, "God is tempting me." For God cannot be tempted by evil, nor does he tempt anyone; but each one is tempted when, by his own evil desire, he is dragged away and enticed.

James 1:13-14

Let not my heart be drawn to what is evil, to take part in wicked deeds.   *Psalm 141:4*

You know with all your heart and soul that not one of all the good promises the Lord your God gave you has failed. Every promise has been fulfilled; not one has failed.   *Joshua 23:14*

The wages of the righteous bring them life but the income of the wicked brings them punishment.

Proverbs 10:16

I am the Lord your God, who teaches you what is best for you, who directs you in the way you should go.   *Isaiah 48:17*

Keep his decrees and commands, which I am giving you today, so that it may go well with you and your children after you.   *Deuteronomy 4:40*

Blessed are they who keep his statutes.

Psalm 119:2

Whoever acknowledges me before men, the Son of Man will also acknowledge him before the angels of God.   *Luke 12:8*

There is rejoicing in the presence of the angels of God over one sinner who repents.

Luke 15:10

I do not hide your righteousness in my heart; I speak of your faithfulness and salvation. I do not conceal your love and your truth from the great assembly.   *Psalm 40:10*

Then the nations will know that I am the Lord, . . . when I show myself holy through you before their eyes.   *Ezekiel 36:23*

All men will know that you are my disciples if you love one another.   *John 13:35*

Do not fear what they fear; do not be frightened. But in your hearts set apart Christ as Lord. Always be prepared to give an answer to everyone who asks you to give the reason for the hope that you have. But do this with gentleness and respect.

1 Peter 3:14-16

I am not ashamed of the gospel, because it is the power of God for the salvation of everyone who believes.   *Romans 1:16*

I declare to you today that I am innocent of the blood of all men. For I have not hesitated to proclaim to you the whole will of God.   *Acts 20:26-27*

How beautiful are the feet of those who bring good news!   *Romans 10:15*

When the Counselor comes, whom I will send to you from the Father, the Spirit of truth who goes out from the Father, he will testify about me; but you also must testify. *John 15:26-27*

Wives, in the same way be submissive to your husbands so that, if any of them do not believe the word, they may be won over without talk by the behavior of their wives.   *1 Peter 3:1*

Believe in the Lord Jesus, and you will be saved— you and your household.   *Acts 16:31*

If a woman has a husband who is not a believer and he is willing to live with her, she must not divorce him. For the unbelieving husband has been sanctified through his wife, and the unbelieving wife has been sanctified through her believing husband. Otherwise your children would be unclean, but as it is they are holy.   *1 Corinthians 7:13-14*

The first thing Andrew did was to find his brother Simon and tell him, "We have found the Messiah. . . ." Then he brought Simon to Jesus.

John 1:41-42

If a wicked man turns away from all the sins he has committed and keeps all my decrees and does what is just and right, he will surely live. . . . Do I take any pleasure in the death of the wicked? declares the Sovereign Lord. Rather, am I not pleased when they turn from their ways and live?   *Ezekiel 18:21-23*

Train a child in the way he should go, and when he is old he will not turn from it.   *Proverbs 22:6*

The Lord is not slow in keeping his promise, as some understand slowness. He is patient with you, not wanting anyone to perish, but everyone to come to repentance.   *2 Peter 3:9*

All your sons will be taught by the Lord.
Isaiah 54:13

Suffering produces perseverance; perseverance, character; and character, hope.   *Romans 5:3-4*

If you should suffer for what is right, you are blessed.   *1 Peter 3:14*

The God of all grace, who called you to his eternal glory in Christ, after you have suffered a little while, will himself restore you and make you strong, firm and steadfast.   *1 Peter 5:10*

Though you have made me see troubles, many and bitter, you will restore my life again.

Psalm 71:20

Shall we accept good from God, and not trouble?

Job 2:10

Dear friends, do not be surprised at the painful trial you are suffering, as though something strange were happening to you. But rejoice that you participate in the sufferings of Christ, so that you may be overjoyed when his glory is revealed.

1 Peter 4:12-13

The Sovereign Lord will wipe away the tears from all faces.   *Isaiah 25:8*

A righteous man may have many troubles, but the Lord delivers him from them all.   *Psalm 34:19*

Let him who walks in the dark, who has no light, trust in the name of the Lord and rely on his God.

Isaiah 50:10

If you suffer for doing good and you endure it, this is commendable before God. To this you were

called, because Christ suffered for you, leaving you an
example, that you should follow in his steps.

1 Peter 2:20-21

I will turn the darkness into light.   *Isaiah 42:16*

When my spirit grows faint within me, it is you who know my way. *Psalm 142:3*

The Lord sustains the humble but casts the wicked to the ground. *Psalm 147:6*

I live in a high and holy place, but also with him who is contrite and lowly in spirit, to revive the spirit of the lowly and to revive the heart of the contrite. *Isaiah 57:15*

The Sovereign Lord is my strength; he makes my feet like the feet of a deer, he enables me to go on the heights. *Habakkuk 3:19*

Look to the Lord and his strength; seek his face always. *1 Chronicles 16:11*

A little while, and the wicked will be no more; though you look for them, they will not be found. But the meek will inherit the land and enjoy great peace. *Psalm 37:10-11*

He ransoms me unharmed from the battle waged against me, even though many oppose me. *Psalm 55:18*

You, O God, are strong, and . . . you, O Lord, are loving. *Psalm 62:11*

He will take pity on the weak and the needy and save the needy from death. *Psalm 72:13*

My grace is sufficient for you, for my power is made perfect in weakness. *2 Corinthians 12:9*

No one is like you, O Lord; you are great, and your name is mighty in power. *Jeremiah 10:6*

I pray that out of his glorious riches he may strengthen you with power through his Spirit in your inner being. *Ephesians 3:16*

DEJECTION

We do not have a high priest who is unable to sympathize with our weaknesses, but we have one who has been tempted in every way, just as we are—yet was without sin. Let us then approach the throne of grace with confidence, so that we may receive mercy and find grace to help us in our time of need.

Hebrews 4:15-16

You will seek me and find me when you seek me with all your heart. *Jeremiah 29:13*

Call to me and I will answer you and tell you great and unsearchable things you do not know.

Jeremiah 33:3

Before they call I will answer; while they are still speaking I will hear. *Isaiah 65:24*

The Spirit helps us in our weakness. We do not know what we ought to pray, but the Spirit himself intercedes for us with groans that words cannot express. And he who searches our hearts knows the mind of the Spirit, because the Spirit intercedes for the saints in accordance with God's will.

Romans 8:26-27

We do not make requests of you because we are righteous, but because of your great mercy.

Daniel 9:18

Come near to God and he will come near to you.

James 4:8

You are kind and forgiving, O Lord, abounding in love to all who call to you. *Psalm 86:5*

I will give them a heart to know me, that I am the Lord. They will be my people, and I will be their God, for they will return to me with all their heart.

Jeremiah 24:7

All you have made will praise you, O Lord; your saints will extol you. *Psalm 145:10*

"Be strong, all you people of the land," declares the Lord, "and work. For I am with you."

Haggai 2:4

Blessed is the man who perseveres under trial, because when he has stood the test, he will receive the crown of life that God has promised to those who love him.

James 1:12

I will bind up the injured and strengthen the weak.

Ezekiel 34:16

He gives strength to the weary and increases the power of the weak.

Isaiah 40:29

My salvation will last forever.

Isaiah 51:6

I thank and praise you, O God of my fathers: You have given me wisdom and power.

Daniel 2:23

The Lord is faithful, and he will strengthen and protect you from the evil one.

2 Thessalonians 3:3

Do not throw away your confidence; it will be richly rewarded.

Hebrews 10:35

Ah, Sovereign Lord, you have made the heavens and the earth by your great power and outstretched arm. Nothing is too hard for you.

Jeremiah 32:17

I pray also that the eyes of your heart may be enlightened in order that you may know the hope to which he has called you.

Ephesians 1:18

God is our refuge and strength, an ever present help in trouble.

Psalm 46:1

Sustain me according to your promise.

Psalm 119:116

The Lord is good and his love endures forever; his faithfulness continues through all generations.

Psalm 100:5

My salvation is on the way.

Isaiah 51:5

Humble yourselves before the Lord, and he will lift you up.
James 4:10

Whom have I in heaven but you? And being with you, I desire nothing on earth. My flesh and my heart may fail, but God is the strength of my heart and my portion forever.
Psalm 73:25-26

I will give you a new heart and put a new spirit in you.
Ezekiel 36:26

The arrogance of man will be brought low and the pride of men humbled.
Isaiah 2:17

"In your anger do not sin": Do not let the sun go down while you are still angry, and do not give the devil a foothold.
Ephesians 4:26-27

My prayer is ever against the deeds of evildoers.
Psalm 141:5

Everyone should be quick to listen, slow to speak and slow to become angry, for man's anger does not bring about the righteous life that God desires.
James 1:19-20

Do nothing out of selfish ambition or vain conceit, but in humility consider others better than yourselves.
Philippians 2:3

The fruit of the Spirit is love, joy, peace, patience, kindness, goodness, faithfulness, gentleness and self-control.
Galatians 5:22-23

You, O Lord, are a compassionate and gracious God, slow to anger, abounding in love and faithfulness.
Psalm 86:15

If a man pays back evil for good, evil will never leave his house.   *Proverbs 17:13*

Trust in him at all times, O people; pour out your hearts to him, for God is our refuge.   *Psalm 62:8*

If you remain in me and my words remain in you, ask whatever you wish, and it will be given you.

John 15:7

You do not have, because you do not ask God. When you ask, you do not receive, because you ask with wrong motives, that you may spend what you get on your own pleasures.   *James 4:2-3*

The Lord is near to all who call on him, to all who call on him in truth.   *Psalm 145:18*

In all things God works for the good of those who love him, who have been called according to his purpose.   *Romans 8:28*

You hear, O Lord, the desire of the afflicted; you encourage them, and you listen to their cry.

Psalm 10:17

If two of you on earth agree about anything you ask for, it will be done for you by my Father in heaven.

Matthew 18:19

If I had cherished sin in my heart, the Lord would not have listened; but God has surely listened and heard my voice in prayer.   *Psalm 66:18-19*

But the eyes of the Lord are on those who fear him, on those whose hope is in his unfailing love.

Psalm 33:18

Whatever you ask for in prayer, believe that you have received it, and it will be yours.   *Mark 11:24*

[God] is able to do immeasurably more than all we ask or imagine, according to his power that is at work within us.   *Ephesians 3:20*

I trust in you, O Lord.   *Psalm 31:14*

When you pass through the waters, I will be with you.
Isaiah 43:2

Precious in the sight of the Lord is the death of his saints.
Psalm 116:15

We do not want you to be ignorant about those who fall asleep, or to grieve like the rest of men, who have no hope. We believe that Jesus died and rose again and so we believe that God will bring with Jesus those who have fallen asleep in him.
1 Thessalonians 4:13-14

But you, O God, do see trouble and grief; you consider it to take it in hand. The victim commits himself to you; you are the helper of the fatherless.
Psalm 10:14

God himself will be with them and be their God. He will wipe every tear from their eyes. There will be no more death or mourning or crying or pain, for the old order of things has passed away.
Revelation 21:3-4

Though you have made me see troubles, many and bitter, you will restore my life again; from the depths of the earth you will again bring me up. You will increase my honor and comfort me once again.
Psalm 71:20-21

If I go and prepare a place for you, I will come back and take you to be with me.
John 14:3

My soul is weary with sorrow; strengthen me according to your word.
Psalm 119:28

May your unfailing love be my comfort, according to your promise to your servant.
Psalm 119:76

Your promise renews my life.
Psalm 119:50

Blessed . . . are those who hear the word of God and obey it. *Luke 11:28*

If any one chooses to do God's will, he will find out whether my teaching comes from God or whether I speak on my own. *John 7:17*

If you obey my commands, you will remain in my love. *John 15:10*

The man who looks intently into the perfect law that gives freedom, and continues to do this, not forgetting what he has heard, but doing it—he will be blessed in what he does. *James 1:25*

If anyone obeys his word, God's love is truly made complete in him. *1 John 2:5*

Everyone who hears these words of mine and puts them into practice is like a wise man who built his house on the rock. *Matthew 7:24*

Direct me in the path of your commands, for there I find delight. *Psalm 119:35*

For the Son of Man is going to come in his Father's glory with his angels, and then he will reward each person according to what he has done.
Matthew 16:27

If anyone loves me, he will obey my teaching. My Father will love him, and we will come to him and make our home with him. *John 14:23*

Blessed are all who fear the Lord, who walk in his ways. *Psalm 128:1*

Jesus said, "If you hold to my teaching, you are really my disciples. Then you will know the truth, and the truth will set you free." *John 8:31-32*

Now I obey your word. *Psalm 119:67*

Now if you obey me fully and keep my covenant, then out of all nations you will be my treasured possession. Although the whole earth is mine, you will be for me a kingdom of priests and a holy nation.

Exodus 19:5-6

We are God's workmanship, created in Christ Jesus to do good works, which God prepared in advance for us to do.

Ephesians 2:10

Now the body [of Christ] is not made up of one part but of many. If the foot should say, "Because I am not a hand, I do not belong to the body," it would not for that reason cease to be part of the body. . . . If the whole body were an eye, where would the sense of hearing be? . . . But in fact God has arranged the parts in the body, every one of them, just as he wanted them to be . . . . Those parts of the body that seem to be weaker are indispensable.

1 Corinthians 12:14-15,17-18, 22

Whoever welcomes this little child in my name welcomes me; and whoever welcomes me welcomes the one who sent me.

Luke 9:48

The man who plants and the man who waters have one purpose, and each will be rewarded according to his own labor. For we are God's fellow workers.

1 Corinthians 3:8-9

Religion that God our Father accepts as pure and faultless is this: to look after orphans and widows in their distress and to keep oneself from being polluted by the world.

James 1:27

Whoever would love life and see good days must keep his tongue from evil and his lips from deceitful speech. He must turn from evil and do good.

1 Peter 3:10-11

My flesh and my heart may fail, but God is the strength of my heart and my portion forever.

Psalm 73:26

I will heal my people and will let them enjoy abundant peace and security. *Jeremiah 33:6*

Is any one of you sick? He should call the elders of the church to pray over him and anoint him with oil in the name of the Lord. And the prayer offered in faith will make the sick person well; the Lord will raise him up. *James 5:14-15*

Heal me, O Lord, and I will be healed; save me and I will be saved, for you are the one I praise.

Jeremiah 17·14

Even though I walk through the valley of the shadow of death, I will fear no evil, for you are with me; your rod and your staff, they comfort me.

Psalm 23:4

Worship the Lord your God, and his blessing will be on your food and water. I will take away sickness from among you, and none will miscarry or be barren in your land. I will give you a full life span.

Exodus 23:25-26

O Lord my God, I called to you for help and you healed me. *Psalm 30:2*

The Lord will sustain him on his sickbed.

Psalm 41:3

May your unfailing love be my comfort, according to your promise to your servant. *Psalm 119:76*

You are a shield around me, O Lord, my Glorious One, who lifts up my head. *Psalm 3:3*

I have seen his ways, but I will heal him; I will guide him and restore comfort to him. *Isaiah 57:18*

Be patient and stand firm, because the Lord's coming is near.
                                                    James 5:8

I am still confident of this: I will see the goodness of the Lord in the land of the living. Wait for the Lord; be strong and take heart and wait for the Lord.
                                              Psalm 27:13-14

In repentance and rest is your salvation, in quietness and trust is your strength.
                                                Isaiah 30:15

Wait for the Lord and keep his way. He will exalt you to possess the land.   *Psalm 37:34*

Be patient, then, brothers, until the Lord's coming. See how the farmer waits for the land to yield its valuable crop and how patient he is for the fall and spring rains. You too, be patient and stand firm.
                                                  James 5:7-8

The suffering and kingdom and patient endurance . . . are ours in Jesus.   *Revelation 1:9*

A man's wisdom gives him patience.
                                              Proverbs 19:11

Those who hope in the Lord will renew their strength.   *Isaiah 40:31*

To those who by persistence in doing good seek glory, honor and immortality, he will give eternal life.
                                                  Romans 2:7

Be still before the Lord and wait patiently for him; do not fret when men succeed in their ways, when they carry out their wicked schemes.
                                                  Psalm 37:7

I was shown mercy so that in me, the worst of sinners, Christ Jesus might display his unlimited patience as an example for those who would believe on him and receive eternal life.   *1 Timothy 1:16*

Blessed are the merciful, for they will be shown mercy. *Matthew 5:7*

Look not only to your own interests, but also to the interests of others. *Philippians 2:4*

[Love] is not easily angered, it keeps no record of wrongs. *1 Corinthians 13:5*

Anyone who speaks against his brother or judges him speaks against the law and judges it. . . . There is only one Lawgiver and Judge, the one who is able to save and destroy. But you—who are you to judge your neighbor? *James 4:11-12*

Love covers over a multitude of sins. *1 Peter 4:8*

If anyone sees his brother commit a sin that does not lead to death, he should pray. *1 John 5:16*

Get rid of all bitterness, rage and anger, brawling and slander, along with every form of malice. Be kind and compassionate to one another, forgiving each other, just as in Christ God forgave you.
Ephesians 4:31-32

Set a guard over my mouth, O Lord; keep watch over the door of my lips. *Psalm 141:3*

Refrain from anger and turn from wrath; do not fret—it leads only to evil. For evil men will be cut off, but those who hope in the Lord will inherit the land.
Psalm 37:8-9

If your brother sins against you, go and show him his fault, just between the two of you. If he listens to you, you have won your brother over. *Matthew 18:15*

[God] will pay back trouble to those who trouble you and give relief to you who are troubled.

2 Thessalonians 1:6-7

My heart's desire and prayer to God . . . is that they may be saved.
Romans 10:1

Holy Father, protect them by the power of your name—the name you gave me—so that they may be one.
John 17:11

Pray for us. We are sure that we have a clear conscience and desire to live honorably in every way.
Hebrews 13:18

I keep asking that the God of our Lord Jesus Christ, the glorious Father, may give you the spirit of wisdom and revelation, so that you may know him better.
Ephesians 1:17

I pray also that . . . you may know the hope to which he has called you, the riches of his glorious inheritance in the saints, and his incomparably great power for us who believe.
Ephesians 1:18-19

And I pray that. . . together with all the saints, [you may know] the love of Christ . . . that surpasses knowledge—that you may be filled to the measure of all the fullness of God.
Ephesians 3:17-19

Pray also for me, that whenever I open my mouth, words may be given me so that I will fearlessly make known the mystery of the gospel.
Ephesians 6:19

This is my prayer: that your love may abound more and more in knowledge and depth of insight, so that you may be able to discern what is best and may be pure and blameless until the day of Christ, filled with the fruit of righteousness that comes through Jesus

Christ—to the glory and praise of God.

Philippians 1:9-11

Let the word of Christ dwell in you.

Colossians 3:16

PART THREE

YOUR PRAYERS ...
GOD'S ANSWERS

The Bible contains many prayers uttered by God's people. These prayers serve as models for us, helping us to express ourselves to the Lord. Scripture is also rich in promises that give us a foretaste of God's answers to our prayers. We may not know when or how God will answer when we cry out to him. But we do know that he hears us, and that he will do what is good for us.

- Our Father in heaven,
- hallowed be your name,
- your kingdom come,
- your will be done
- on earth as it is in heaven.
- Give us today our daily bread.
- Forgive us our debts,
- as we also have forgiven our debtors.
- And lead us not into temptation,
- but deliver us from the evil one.

Matthew 6:9-13

- God reigns over the nations; God is seated on his holy throne. *Psalm 47:8*
- The God of heaven will set up a kingdom that will never be destroyed. *Daniel 2:44*
- The sovereignty, power and greatness of the kingdoms under the whole heaven will be handed over to the saints, the people of the Most High. His kingdom will be an everlasting kingdom, and all rulers will worship and obey him. *Daniel 7:27*
- He provides food for those who fear him; he remembers his covenant forever. *Psalm 111:5*
- I will cleanse them from all the sin they have committed against me and will forgive all their sins of rebellion against me. *Jeremiah 33:8*
- God cannot be tempted by evil, nor does he tempt anyone. *James 1:13*
- You, dear children, are from God and have overcome them, because the one who is in you is greater than the one who is in the world. *1 John 4:4*

- Rescue me, O Lord, from evil men; protect me from men of violence. *Psalm 140:1*
- Let the wicked fall into their own nets, while I pass by in safety. *Psalm 141:10*
- Make us glad for as many days as you have afflicted us, for as many years as we have seen trouble. *Psalm 90:15*
- Summon your power, O God; show us your strength, O God, as you have done before.
  Psalm 68:28
- According to your great compassion blot out my transgressions. Wash away all my iniquity and cleanse me from my sin. *Psalm 51:1-2*
- Do not bring your servant into judgment, for no one living is righteous before you.
  Psalm 143:2
- I have been disciplined. Restore me, and I will return. *Jeremiah 31:18*
- Teach me knowledge and good judgment, for I believe in your commands. *Psalm 119:66*

- Fear of man will prove to be a snare, but whoever trusts in the Lord is kept safe.

  Proverbs 29:25

- The faithless will be fully repaid for their ways, and the good man rewarded for his.

  Proverbs 14:14

- I will repay you for the years the locusts have eaten. *Joel 2:25*

- In the time of my favor I will answer you, and in the day of salvation I will help you.

  Isaiah 49:8

- As far as the east is from the west, so far has he removed our transgressions from us.

  Psalm 103:12

- The Lord is gracious and compassionate, slow to anger and rich in love. *Psalm 145:8*

- Make every effort to live in peace with all men and to be holy; without holiness no one will see the Lord. *Hebrews 12:14*

- Now that you know these things, you will be blessed if you do them. *John 13:17*

- I seek you with all my heart; do not let me stray from your commands.   *Psalm 119:10*
- Lord, listen! O Lord, forgive! O Lord, hear and act! For your sake, O my God, do not delay.
  Daniel 9:19
- Let the morning bring me word of your unfailing love, for I have put my trust in you.
  Psalm 143:8
- Let the heads of those who surround me be covered with the trouble their lips have caused.
  Psalm 140:9
- Arise, Lord! Lift up your hand, O God. Do not forget the helpless.   *Psalm 10:12*
- I confess my iniquity; I am troubled by my sin.
  Psalm 38:18
- O righteous God, who searches minds and hearts, bring to an end the violence of the wicked and make the righteous secure.
  Psalm 7:9
- Teach me to do your will.   *Psalm 143:10*
- Restore to me the joy of your salvation and grant me a willing spirit, to sustain me.
  Psalm 51:12

- I will put my Spirit in you and move you to follow my decrees. *Ezekiel 36:27*
- I will heal their waywardness and love them freely. *Hosea 14:4*
- I tell you the truth, until heaven and earth disappear, not the smallest letter, not the least stroke of a pen, will by any means disappear from the Law until everything is accomplished. *Matthew 5:18*
- I will punish the world for its evil, the wicked for their sins. *Isaiah 13:11*
- They will live securely, for then his greatness will reach to the ends of the earth. And he will be their peace. *Micah 5:4*
- Return faithless people; I will cure you of backsliding. *Jeremiah 3:22*
- He will judge the world in righteousness and the peoples in his truth. *Psalm 96:13*
- I have set before you life and death, blessings and curses. Now choose life, . . . love the Lord your God, listen to his voice, and hold fast to him. For the Lord is your life. *Deuteronomy 30:19-20*
- The Lord will establish you as his holy people, as he promised you on oath, if you keep the commands of the Lord your God and walk in his ways. *Deuteronomy 28:9*

- I am in pain and distress; may your salvation, O God, protect me. *Psalm 69:29*
- Lead me, O Lord, in your righteousness because of my enemies—make straight your way before me. *Psalm 5:8*
- Do not be far from me, for trouble is near and there is no one to help. *Psalm 22:11*
- Remember not the sins of my youth and my rebellious ways; according to your love remember me, for you are good, O Lord.
  Psalm 25:7
- Do not cast me away when I am old; do not forsake me when my strength is gone.
  Psalm 71:9
- Teach us to number our days aright, that we may gain a heart of wisdom. *Psalm 90:12*
- Turn to me and be gracious to me, for I am lonely and afflicted. *Psalm 25:16*
- But may all who seek you rejoice and be glad in you. *Psalm 70:4*
- Save us and help us with your right hand, that those you love may be delivered. *Psalm 60:5*
- Hear my prayer, O Lord, listen to my cry for help. *Psalm 39:12*

- Our God is a God who saves.   *Psalm 68:20*
- Whoever lives by the truth comes into the light.   *John 3:21*
- I will be faithful and righteous to them as their God.   *Zechariah 8:8*
- If you repent, I will restore you that you may serve me.   *Jeremiah 15:19*
- They will still bear fruit in old age, they will stay fresh and green, proclaiming, "The Lord is upright."   *Psalm 92:14-15*
- Be faithful, even to the point of death, and I will give you the crown of life.

           Revelation 2:10
- I will rejoice in doing them . . . good.

           Jeremiah 32:41
- They will celebrate your abundant goodness and joyfully sing of your righteousness.

           Psalm 145:7
- All mankind will fear; they will proclaim the works of God and ponder what he has done.

           Psalm 64:9
- The Lord has heard my cry for mercy; the Lord accepts my prayer.   *Psalm 6:9*

I will declare that your love stands firm forever, that you established your faithfulness in heaven itself.

Psalm 89:2

My whole being will exclaim, "Who is like you, O Lord?"
Psalm 35:10

I will praise you, O Lord, among the nations; I will sing of you among the peoples. For great is your love, reaching to the heavens; your faithfulness reaches to the skies.
Psalm 57:9-10

But I will sing of your strength, in the morning I will sing of your love; for you are my fortress, my refuge in times of trouble.
Psalm 59:16

O my Strength, I sing praise to you; you, O God, are my fortress, my loving God.
Psalm 59:17

Then will I ever sing praise to your name and fulfill my vows day after day.
Psalm 61:8

I will praise you as long as I live, and in your name I will lift up my hands.
Psalm 63:4

Because you are my help, I sing in the shadow of your wings.
Psalm 63:7

Praise be to God, who has not rejected my prayer or withheld his love from me!
Psalm 66:20

Now to the King eternal, immortal, invisible, the only God, be honor and glory for ever and ever.

1 Timothy 1:17

I will proclaim the name of the Lord. Oh, praise the greatness of our God! He is the Rock, his works are perfect, and all his ways are just. A faithful God who does no wrong, upright and just is he.

Deuteronomy 32:3-4

You are mighty, O Lord.
Psalm 89:8

How great are your works, O Lord, how profound your thoughts! *Psalm 92:5*

I will sing to the Lord all my life; I will sing praise to my God as long as I live. *Psalm 104:33*

I love you, O Lord, my strength. *Psalm 18:1*

I praise you because I am fearfully and wonderfully made; your works are wonderful. *Psalm 139:14*

Great is the Lord and most worthy of praise; his greatness no one can fathom. *Psalm 145:3*

I will praise you, O Lord. Although you were angry with me, your anger has turned away and you have comforted me. *Isaiah 12:1*

O great and powerful God, whose name is the Lord Almighty, great are your purposes and mighty are your deeds. *Jeremiah 32:18-19*

You are awesome, O God, in your sanctuary; . . . Praise be to God! *Psalm 68:35*

My soul praises the Lord and my spirit rejoices in God my Savior. *Luke 1:46-47*

I will sing of the love of the Lord forever; with my mouth I will make your faithfulness known through all generations. I will declare that your love stands firm forever, that you established your faithfulness in heaven itself. *Psalm 89:1-2*

You are worthy, our Lord and God, to receive glory and honor and power, for you created all things, and by your will they were created and have their being. *Revelation 4:11*

Give thanks to the Lord for he is good; his love endures forever.   *Psalm 107:1*